Childhood Sexual Abuse: "You are a bright light on this planet." BS

Survivors of Abuse: "I am letting you know the part you play in encouragement and healing." RG

Effects of Child Abuse: "Keep writing! It gives others hope." MG

Healing Abuse: "It is reassuring to know I am not alone." DF

Abuse Recovery: "Your writing is so powerful." MD

Abuse Survivors: "Thank you for the great work you do to help survivors heal and be heard." ~ Gretchen Paules of LetGoLetPeaceComeIn.org

This book is for

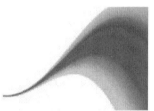

Survivors of childhood sexual abuse who want to reclaim who they are beneath the layers of their experience.

Friends and family of survivors who want to empower the healing journeys of people they love.

Readers who are always ready to celebrate resilient personal spirit and empowerment.

Healing allies who are looking for gentle, encouraging insights for those they are helping.

Jeanne McElvaney is all about the beauty and power of resilient personal spirit. For the past 40 years, she has been celebrating, exploring, and writing about the wonder of this force. A master of language and feelings, her fiction is often a *journey of insight.* Her practical, empowering, gentle and healing insights for survivors of childhood sexual abuse come from her heart and her own experience.

Warmed by family connections and rich friendships, she lives in California where her awesomely supportive husband and delightfully distracting dog live in *possibilities.*

"Jeanne has an uncanny ability to help people see more clearly what is happening to them." ~ SK

Other books by Jeanne McElvaney

Spirit Unbroken: Abby's Story ~ this novel will take you to the core of dissociated memories as Abby's innocent childhood successes are woven into her sexual abuse.

☆.•° Finalist in Readers Favorite Awards - Women's Fiction .•° ☆

Childhood Abuse ~ a gentle, inspiring, self help, empowerment guide for survivors of childhood sexual abuse

Harrietta's Happenstance ~ a sweet romance floating on the surface of sexual abuse issues (Paddington Cove Series)

Old Maggie's Spirit Whispers ~ this story of unusual friendships celebrates inner wisdom guiding everyday choices (Paddington Cove Series)

Time Slipping ~ Elizabeth's retreat to discover who she is outside her responsibilities, relationships, and routines grabs the reader for their own journey of insight (Paddington Cover Series)

Personal Development Insights ~ with intuition, energy conversations, and courage, we can go anywhere.

Table of Contents

Black-Ink Insights

"The Power of Art in Healing'
Queen Emma Art Gallery – Honolulu, HI

Healing Insights

31 Empowering, Gentle Choices for Change
&
15 Black-Ink Healing Images

By
Jeanne McElvaney

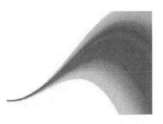

1 ~ IT DOESN'T

"JUST GO AWAY"

There is a moment in our healing journey when our denial crumbles and we realize our experience and its continued effects on us won't "just go away." That's our breakthrough moment. It's the sun coming out to warm the seeds of hope so they can grow our personal garden of empowerment.

Though our childhood sexual abuse affects every moment of every day, we are inclined to ignore our truth for many good reasons. Embracing it threatens change and asks us to make ourselves as important as others. To honor our truth, we have to quiet our lives so we can travel inward where our memories can be comprehended. Accepting it means trusting our feelings though we have learned to suppress them and our perceptions to protect ourselves. Exploring our truth challenges us to recognize we can find our way when we feel so lost.

Denial comes in all shapes and sizes. Holding the past on the other side of awareness, it becomes our ally in building our lives. Avoiding the deep, dark holes of abuse memories helped us get to here-and-now. Acknowledging them opens the door to healing. Choosing to look into those holes allows us to find new paths into our future.

Our abuse doesn't "just go away." It's recorded in every cell of our body. Every choice we make is shaped by our experience. What we believe about the world and how we fit in its possibilities came from those moments when we felt powerless.

When we are ready to reach for days that honor our spirit, we can face our denial, knowing our abuse doesn't define us. When we are ready to embrace our dreams, we will recognize avoidance is simply the tired and worn defense we used to help us get by.

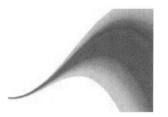

2 ~ RELEASING GUILT

Guilt isn't the child of logic or reason. It's not easily dislodged with information. This invasive adversary grew like a vine during my childhood sexual abuse and had a second spurt of growth in my active healing years.

As I did the courageous work of going back into my dissociated memories, guilt seemed to wait in the corner of nearly every experience.

I found it tangled in misplaced shame. Not able to separate myself from the violation of hands I needed to trust, I accepted blame as though I were responsible for the betrayal. Unable to comprehend what was happening, I assumed I was a partner in the crime against my body. Guilt was the slime that settled in because the alternative, knowing I was absolutely powerless, was unbearable.

Back then, I felt guilty for not being normal like my friends. I laughed when they did, agreed to go where they wanted, and hid behind excuses when I didn't know to be part of their world. It wasn't my own curiosity or inner wisdom that led the way. My choices were guided by my need to fit in so my shame wouldn't be visible.

In my healing journey, I felt like I was releasing layers upon layers of guilt. Retrieving memories gave me this opportunity, but I found myself visited by new guilt. Like the guilt from my past, these feelings also had to be recognized, acknowledged, and released.

It was challenging to let go of the discomfort I felt about the way my healing disrupted my days as a mother and wife. It took a garden full of praise and encouragement from my kids, husband, sister, and therapist to pull one weed of guilt.

And I had to face the guilt I felt for 'not being who I thought I was' when I married my husband. I felt less. He celebrated me for being more.

There was also the guilt of change. Healing transformed my world. Rather than trying to have a picnic in a dark, dense, forest with storm clouds in every direction, I had moved to a sunny meadow filled with wildflower possibilities. That meant giving up the activities, beliefs, and people who could only share the forest with me… those relationships that needed me to remain who I had become to survive.

In the many layers of guilt attached to my abuse, the greatest remorse, the one that brought me to my knees, hit me as my first memory emerged: I hadn't protected my sister. I now know I was powerless to do that; healing has given me the opportunity to soothe that guilt. Now I can reach out to others and make a difference. I can be a voice to stop the cycle of abuse that hides behind secrets and silence.

Each survivor has something to pass forward to others. We often find that during our healing journey.

3 ~ I'M MORE THAN MY ABUSE

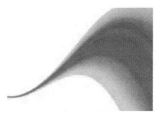

It takes Superman courage and Wonder Woman determination to heal the wounds of childhood sexual abuse. That choice comes with change. And though there are compelling reasons to invite this renewal, we are also inclined to hold on dearly to whatever stability we have created out of the chaos of our past experience.

I was one of the 50% who dissociated my traumatic memories. When those flashbacks began crashing into my days, it left my life in pieces. I didn't feel I had any choice but to seek help and healing. It promised understanding and reprieve. I had no idea it would also bring gifts.

The shame, fears, and powerlessness from my abuse had left me feeling one-dimensional. In a world of shining possibilities, I had learned how to appear NORMAL, but only if I kept my life small. It took my healing journey to show me that who I had become in order to manage my trauma was not who I was.

As I opened up the door to my truth, I discovered so much more than my childhood circumstance. There in the corners were facets of "me" that had been buried. Reclaiming my truth empowered me. Telling my story made it possible to quit reading the same chapters over and over; I was able to start exploring new chapters in my life. Saving the "little girls" within, who were still caught in the timeless web of my abuse, revealed talents and abilities I'd never imagined. Feeling safe for the first time in my life opened new vistas of personal passion and purpose.

In healing, I found I am more than my abuse.

I would be the first to urge survivors to embrace their own healing journey to bring peace, empowerment, and stability into their lives. But there is much more. Healing can also reveal the inner you that got overwhelmed by what was happening in your everyday world. It will shine a light on your rich possibilities.

4 ~ ANGER

During my healing, anger was a challenging, elusive, frightening emotion for me. Growing up, I had witnessed it blowing up without apparent reason. I had seen it used to terrify, exploit, and cower. It had soaked into the fabric of my family until it dampened even the sunniest moments.

I grew up believing anger was a malignancy I wanted to avoid at all costs. Though I couldn't stop it in others, I became a powerful sheriff arresting any lawless anger that threatened to escape in my own reactions. I learned how to capture it and put it away without recognizing it had dared to threaten my thoughts.

I learned to cope by completely shutting down this emotion, but healing asks us to find our way back to our authentic self. It acknowledges all feelings are a gift of self-awareness when we learn how to express them in ways that honor our relationships.

I had to dig deep to find my anger. Recognizing it would bring insight, I invited it, even begged myself to have the courage to be with that emotion and trust it wouldn't destroy me or those I loved. One day, I realized I needed to see this old enemy if I was going to make it my friend. It was a jagged, dark, darting force, but the drawing showed me it couldn't destroy. It was contained by waves of my spirit.

Step by step, I became reacquainted with this very natural, necessary emotion. First I recognized it. Then I wrote about it. One day, I expressed it! I felt like I was blowing the roof off my life, but my husband and kids told me I had done nothing more than raise my voice and express my feelings. We celebrated my huge breakthrough.

While I had to uncover my anger, I know other survivors feel it has been a persistent, stormy presence in their reactions. We have to travel from different directions to embrace its empowering possibilities, but I believe anger is a worthy ally. It's a road sign to guide us and help us take care of ourselves. It shows up to tell us we have come to a circumstance that does not honor our spirit. It asks us to set new, uncomfortable boundaries.

5 ~ MY SEA OF BLACK TEARS

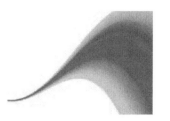

Many of us resist tears when feelings threaten to take us back to our past abuse. Convinced they will never stop once we let them through the dam, we rely on old ways of managing our discomfort.

I was sure the tears that knew everything about my childhood sexual abuse would carry me out to sea. I couldn't imagine it was possible to simply wade in the emotions asking me to cry. The pain was too deep. Betrayal was too agonizing. Guilt, confusion, and fear were bottomless.

But, as healing took me to my truth, I became stronger. One day, my tears recognized I was ready. They came to me when I had a quiet afternoon to myself. I didn't resist though I was convinced my kids and husband would arrive home to find nothing but a still-sobbing puddle.

I discovered tears aren't the bottom of the sea where I would drown. They are the waves. In a moment of welling emotion, they might carry me like a tidal wave, but they are always heading for the steady shore. In my healing journey, crying became as constant as the surf, but I was never pulled out to sea.

When I was no longer afraid of the tears, when I embraced their value, I discovered they came to support me. These tears did not come to rub my wound. They brought relief so my injuries could heal. They didn't come to wash me away with a memory. They brought insight and clues about my experience so I could change my life.

In my sea of black tears, I found I could swim toward the day when my abuse no longer defined my life.

6 ~ CONFUSION

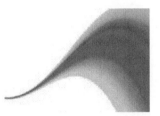

Learning about life in a cauldron of childhood sexual abuse leaves survivors with simmering confusion. Many of our impressions and beliefs about ourselves were born in psychological chaos. We arrived at adulthood too wise and achingly innocent. We began traveling down that path carrying a backpack of misconceptions.

Our sexuality was surely twisted and often crumbled into pieces. What should have been left for our own exploration, timing, and choices was ripped out of our control. Many of us were required to participate before we could fathom adult physical intimacy. Some of us were trapped by fear or the power and authority of our abuser. Others had their very innocent, normal desire for affection exploited.

All of us were tossed into deep, stormy waters before we knew how to swim. We didn't know how we got there or why. We didn't know how to reach shore. And so we did what we could; we swam in circles of confusion trying to stay afloat.

Our bodies also held a mountain of confusion. Some of us were taught our looks caused the distorted attention we received. Others learned they were powerless to save themselves. We hated our abusers and, just as often, hated our bodies for being the object that caused so much pain. In the bewildering world of our abuse, we didn't have the opportunity to learn how to take care of *"THE HOUSE"* we live in.

Love was another casualty of the confusion we experienced. Our abusers might not have been part of our family, but 90% of them were known and trusted. Where we should have found safety, care, celebration, and protection, we experienced betrayal. We were used under the banner of affection. As a child, it became part of the flavor we associated with love. Then it often soured into repeating, perplexing choices we made in the years that followed.

Our childhood sexual abuse set the stage for a confusing cast of characters and dramas. Our healing journeys offer us insights so we can re-write the play about our sensuality and love.

7 ~ THE OTHER SIDE
OF HEALING

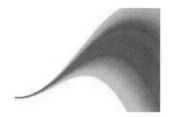

If I had a magic wand, I would wave away the very natural and usual resistance we have about healing from our childhood sexual abuse. I know our experience holds us down though we think ignoring it makes us feel steady. I also know gifts will come with each step we take.

I wish I was a fairy godmother equal to Cinderella's, waving my wand so every survivor could ride their own pumpkin carriage to the other side of healing, feeling confident they would be going to the glitter and joy of their authentic selves.

Cinderella's reward for daring to imagine there was more came with the perfect fit of a glass slipper. It took her to love and a future of promise. We also have glass slippers waiting for us. Each one will be a perfect fit when we are on the other side of healing.

During our abuse, we accepted any shoes that helped us survive the journey. They got us out of that time, but they took us to destinations that very often didn't feel like a good fit. It can be the way we eat, days that are too busy, circumstances that overwhelm, jobs that diminish, and love that hurts. These ill-fitting shoes often took us to beliefs about trust, self-esteem, and happiness that twist our choices.

Healing asks us to take those shoes off and walk barefoot on paths that reveal our experience so we are empowered by information and understanding. When we quit avoiding so we can update the information trapped in our abuse, we are empowered. Only then can we slip on the glass slipper that feels like a perfect fit so we can dance with life without blisters.

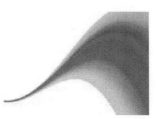

8 ~ EMPOWERED SELF

AWARENESS

In the exploding, imploding, lonely moments of our childhood abuse, our sense of feeling safe in the world was mortally wounded. Yet our resilient spirit helped us survive by conjuring ways we could take action to protect ourselves in the future.

These ready responses and instinctive reactions become our magic wands. We used them in all situations, regardless if they were appropriate and whether they truly served us. Like sticking our tongue out when we were bullied, they made us feel better.

To feel safe in my life, I became hypervigilant. I developed a *"SONAR ABILITY"* to track everyone within sight or sound. I believed I knew what they were thinking, feeling, and needing. And I developed another magic wand to go with this; I believed I could make my life safe if I was always a good, thoughtful, and helpful girl.

These two magic wands are common to survivors. And we share a long list of other traits we developed so we could feel in control. Though they got us from back-then to here-and-now, these coping responses were smoke screens of safety.

Having authentic choices in every moment of every day is our strongest protection. It is one thing to be "good, thoughtful, and helpful" by choice and another thing entirely if I feel compelled by past beliefs to show up this way in every circumstance.

Feeling safe isn't just about leaving our abuser behind. It's about discovering what drives our reactions so we know if they have roots in our childhood trauma. It is digging into our past so we can be confident our current reactions are coming from empowered, self-aware choices.

9 ~ PERSONAL SPIRIT AND CHILDHOOD SEXUAL ABUSE

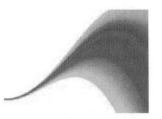

In our childhood abuse, we learned to place our focus on our abusers. Living with constant uncertainty, we watched their moods to gauge our reactions. Faced with the physical and emotional pain they created, their feelings became more important than ours. We turned ourselves inside-out trying to understand them so we could try to create normal days out of chaos. We accepted their shame as our own. Worried about our survival, we listened to their reasons for silence.

We did the best we could in the shadows of childhood by becoming experts about our abusers. We didn't know our connection to our personal spirit was a casualty.

Our spirit was there during our abuse. It made it possible for us to live, learn, love, and laugh in spite of the dark corners in our days. But as we turned the force of our attention on our abusers, our chance to hear its guiding messages or feel the gentle nudges were greatly diminished.

Healing brings a new relationship with our spirit. While our abuse gave us no choices, the journey to well-being calls on us to make choices every step of the way. Every time we choose, reject, turn down one path or pick another path, we are empowering ourselves. Those choices come from our inner wisdom… the seat of our personal spirit.

Learning to turn to our self rather than our abuser for information, we begin shaping our days and our future with our personal spirit guiding. This connection grows stronger until we can walk off an elevator because someone *"JUST DOESN'T FEEL RIGHT"*. Or we can follow a feeling that leads us to the perfect book, song, movie, moment, person, and insight to move our healing forward.

Healing from childhood sexual abuse brings many gifts to us. Being vibrantly, constantly in touch with our personal spirit is surely one of them.

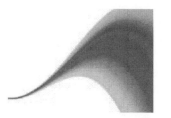

10 ~ RELEASING SHAME

I'm convinced we can't escape our childhood sexual abuse without shame. It sticks to us no matter how much we achieve and in spite of loving relationships. This disempowering feeling is one of the big challenges in healing... which means it also holds some of our richest insights to help us live our potential.

A hundred people can tell us this shame is not ours, that it belongs to our abusers. And they are right, but it doesn't seem to diminish the swirl of humiliating disgrace and guilt we feel. Logic doesn't erase the inner recording that has us convinced we deserve the label pinned to our identity.

For me, healing this misplaced belief about myself meant going back to the moment shame seeped into my being and took root. With the help of my therapist, I was able to go beyond remembering. I got to see the circumstance in context... through the eyes of childhood, trauma, powerlessness, and betrayal. That's when I could see the shame I had taken forward was not mine.

It was a daring journey, but I never carried the shame again. I had chosen to leave it with my abuser.

As my healing continued and different shades of shame would occasionally reach out for me, I learned to send it back by using imagery. I saw my shame as muddy, green slime. I would imagine grabbing it and throwing it back on my abuser until he was buried. Then I would stand tall in my new awareness, inviting sparkles of my possibilities to fill the air around me.

11 ~ HEALING: HOW LONG

DOES IT TAKE ?

Healing from our childhood sexual abuse calls to us in odd moments. It's like a whisper as we once again pass by an old gate on the familiar road we've been traveling.

The path on the other side of the gate is overgrown with memories we've dissociated or tried to ignore. The unmapped landscape beyond is heavy with stormy weather, but hope urges us to lift the latch. The desire to have more in our life invites us to step toward the promise of understanding, release, and new possibilities.

The question that comes up as we open the gate is: how long will this take?

This is a valid question. It acknowledges the uncertainties of such a journey. It recognizes our new focus and intention will transform our days. The question admits our healing will pull other people into the dark mystery that has kidnapped our lives.

When I chose to heal, I was hungry for an answer about how long I would be wrapped around such a deep, very personal, confusing issue. Not finding an answer from others, I decided I could do anything for three months. Thinking I couldn't possibly manage more than that, I was willing to ask my family, friends, and my self to let go of "what was" for "what could be" for twelve weeks. In a maze of turmoil and trust, I gave myself a destination.

It took much longer but, after three months, time no longer mattered. My journey unfolded in spirit-miles as I found answers that let me release how I managed my life and relationships so I could discover how to blow on the bubbles of a joyful life.

Healing is never over, but there comes a time when it is just an occasional summer storm that you welcome because it nurtures what you're planting. The desire to know 'how long it will take' slips away because you realize you aren't taking a detour that will lead back to the familiar path you traveled for so many years.

When you go through the gate, you are heading in a new direction where gifts and treasures will be found along the way, where healing is another word for embracing your potential for happiness.

12 ~ THE POWER OF IMAGES

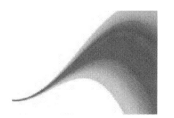

During sexual abuse, we were pulled into a dimension beyond our capacity to comprehend. Though we found our way back to the everyday world and often appeared "normal," we continued to feel branded. An ominous sensation followed us into our adult years.

Some of us feel a darkness hovering. Many sense a ticking bomb. There are survivors who remain in a constant state of flight and those who are numb. Identifying the over-all feeling we brought out of abusive experiences can empower our healing.

My abuse left me feeling like I was alone in the deepest corner of a dark forest. No sunlight reached the overgrown spot where I lay curled up and lost. There was no path out. When my first memory blew my world apart, that is what I saw. As my healing journey began, I also saw an open, sunny meadow at the edge of my forest; my challenge was to find my way to the light.

This image sustained me. It gave me something solid to focus on during a process that feels so circular, bewildering, and frightening. With this picture in mind, I saw each challenge as tangled vines. Each choice to embrace my truth felt like I was slashing through the under growth of secrets and creating a path.

I recognized there was no map, but I imagined my allies carrying torches and walking beside me.

Every time I dared to reclaim a memory, I believed I was saving a child I'd left behind, and I would bring her out of the memory to walk beside me. Both of us became stronger as I "listened" her insights and feelings as we continued our journey out of the forest.

Creating an image that represents our healing journey can make all the difference. Whether it's sailing to a safe island in an ocean of confusion or sewing a quilt from the patches of painful memories, it offers comfort. Any image can be an empowering tool as long as it has deep meaning to the survivor who is finding their way.

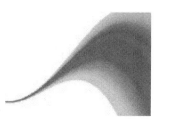

13 ~ THE GIFTS OF HEALING

Survivors of childhood sexual abuse often feel tremendous resistance to stepping onto the path of active healing. The dragons of our experience feel too large and overwhelming even when we are told we will find incredible, empowering, joy-filled, peaceful days on the other side of healing.

While I fully embrace each survivor's choices with an open heart, I want to keep shining the light on the tremendous rewards found in healing journeys. This week, I was reminded of these gifts when another dragon came roaring out of nowhere.

It swooped into a dream that had all the signs of a fragmented memory. I woke up thinking, "I used my voice! I used my voice!" Oh, that was a glorious first, but I was also stunned because this was not my primary abuser. I was being shown another pond of slime in a landscape I thought I knew.

This memory came at a time when I was facing a big choice. One path would take me back toward the comfortable and familiar. The other one would challenge my strong beliefs about what I couldn't have or didn't deserve. With this decision haunting me, I chose to set aside the memory. It came back the next morning when I woke up in a dizzy, adrenalized state.

While my thoughts and feelings encouraged me to ignore the messenger, by body was urging me toward insight. The moment I actively chose to follow the clues being offered, the answer about which path to take became clear. The choice felt good and strong; I am going to embrace the challenging opportunity, the one that will open doors.

I haven't completed my journey with this new memory, but it has already given me an empowering gift. That is always true in our healing process; we are offered treasures along the way. Without knowing the details, I already know this past experience is linked to ways I have held myself back. If the memory hadn't nudged me, if I hadn't listened and responded, my abuse would have been the force behind my decision. I would have chosen the safe path… and missed a chance to grow my life in a way that will celebrate my spirit.

14 ~ WHAT IS MY TRUTH?

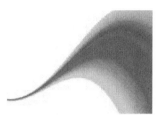

A survivor of childhood sexual abuse recently shared the struggle she feels between what her heart feels and what her head tells her. She asked if I had that experience.

Absolutely! And leaving this tug and pull behind is surely one of the empowering gifts of healing from our trauma. We discover there is a third place to go for our answers: one that is sure and honors our personal truth. I call it our spirit.

Our head definitely wants to take charge of any answers because it was a strong ally during our abuse. Within the maze of incomprehensible circumstances, our logic wove explanations that would help us survive. During healing, we can honor our mind for conjuring these empowering beliefs even as we see they were the thoughts of a child in the midst of trauma. Back then, they had helped us carry on. Today, they may not be the best guide.

Though our hearts were being battered, they are surely our badge of courage. In the shadows of our days, they gave us a steady beat that was connected to the music of personal connections. They led us to all the reasons we could believe in the bright possibilities of life.

Our spirit was always present, but this inner wisdom that holds our personal truth had no place to be expressed during our abuse. We lost our confident, conscious connection to that place inside that "just knows." While our head is swayed by experiences and our heart is influenced by the desire for love, our spirit holds our truth as a gentle map to our purpose and potential.

Healing journeys rarely give us facts and confirmation, but we have something even more powerful: our spirit. We get to ask ourselves, "What do I *just know* beyond logic and feelings? What's *my* truth?" We are empowered by asking this… and then trusting the answers that come to us.

15 ~ EMPOWERING TEARS

For survivors, the past is a landscape of memories and feelings we want to avoid. Though there are moments of nostalgia scattered through those days, we have to tread lightly so we don't consciously bump into reminders of our childhood sexual abuse. Avoiding tears is one way we keep those experiences at bay.

Back then, crying made us feel weak and made no difference. Our emotional and physical pain could be flowing across our cheeks, but that didn't stop the trauma. Eyes could fill as utter powerlessness held us captive and our abuser looked the other way. Fist-clenching, stomping, and stormy anger was often found on wet pillows.

When we were caught in the web of our abuse, tears escaped while we tightly wrapped our arms around ourselves, knowing we were on our own. Now they can be something quite different. They can be partners in our healing.

Wherever we are on this empowering journey, tears are an ally. Every time we "feel like crying," we have discovered a piece of our experience ready to be released. Holding the tears might numb our awareness, but following the feelings to insights will help us build a future where our abuse is no longer guiding our choices and responses.

Many of us have held the tears for so long, we think they will never stop if we open the gate, but holding them in is a forever-ache. Letting them come can be measured in minutes and hours. Letting them flow freely can wash away the emotion that was trapped in our abuse.

Our tears are a tool in our healing journeys. By finding the best time and place to let them flow, we are following the trail back to who we are beyond the storms of our abuse. In time, tears of release will turn into tears of joy.

16 ~ COURAGE OF NEW

CHOICES

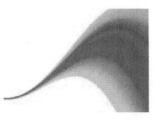

We do it so often... and so well. We think understanding why someone abused us diminishes its effect on us. This is a disempowering web for survivors of childhood sexual abuse.

Although it gives us the comfort of not upsetting other people, excusing our abuser because we understand them keeps us firmly trapped in our experience.

Drinking, anger, exhaustion or depression can never, ever be an adequate reason for harming us.

If our abuser was also a victim at one time, he/she needed to seek help rather than use our childhood vulnerability as an opportunity to violate us.

Not "knowing what they were doing" or "recognizing how much it affected us" denies responsibility and asks us to carry the load.

There is no amount of understanding that will make things better, even when we think we are doing something good. It doesn't rock the boat, but our good intention keeps us tied to all the ways our abuse continues to affect our choices, health, and happiness. It strangles any effort to heal the wounds of our abuse.

"Understanding" lets us keep our secret, but it protects our abuser and leaves us with our scars.

One empowering tool for healing is… recognizing we can understand our abuser and still make them responsible for their actions.

This empowering change creates shifts in how we feel about ourselves and that changes how others treat us. When insight about our abuse becomes a beacon of truth, we have a new guide for our choices. That's when we can honor our mind~body~spirit.

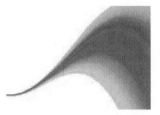

17 ~ COURAGE TO CHANGE

OUR RELATIONSHIPS

The lessons we learn as children shape our choices many years later. For those who experienced childhood sexual abuse, this influence was ramped up and tied to our sense of survival. We left home armed with the same instinctive responses that helped us manage the chaos of our youth.

Believing we have to accept all relationships is one of these impulses. We didn't grow up learning how to discern, choose, initiate, or decline associations with other people. Like fly paper, we were stuck with anyone who chose to get near us.

Our healing journey shows us this is no longer true. Though we can't change how people treat us, we get to choose who we invite into our days. We aren't fly paper. We're butterflies in a garden of potential relationships. We get to land on flowering possibilities that are right for us and move away from the blossoms that don't feel good.

Every day, every moment, we now have the power to decide who enriches our lives. Using this information, we can create a web of relationships that support our dreams, celebrate our spirit, and share a journey of personal growth.

Healing takes us away from "have to" and "should." It reminds us to move out of relationships whenever we feel diminished by the connection. It helps us recognize bonds that have us repeating hurtful patterns we knew in the past. It gives us the courage to embrace those who will nurture our future.

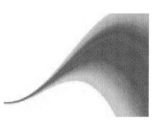

18 ~ SELF HELP SNUGGLED

INTO SELF AWARENESS

Childhood sexual abuse severely diminishes self awareness. Ask a survivor what other people need from them and you will get an instantaneous, perceptive, clear listing. We are tuned into this as though our life depended on it. And it often did.

This ability to know what makes others comfortable and happy with us does not translate into recognizing what we need to feel good. That information is like wood shavings on the floor as we carve our choices around expectations in our relationships. Yet there is great empowerment in identifying what makes us smile, sigh, and soar.

Wherever we are in our healing journey, it's hugely helpful to make a list of what feels good and right. We are empowered when we know what feels like a fit or makes our days better and life seem sweet. If you are like me, this first effort will name old and new dreams. It will shine a light on events. We tend to see what we want as the 'sometime moments' we've imagined or those we experience now and then.

These are great, but they're only part of the story. The list for really changing our lives is about the little things that make all the difference: wearing a favorite pair of pants, looking out our kitchen window, or the snap and crunch of a cold apple. When we honor the every day, very personal things that make us feel good, we invite happiness. And we're in charge of it.

The mirror that was cracked during our abuse still holds the perfect image of our unique self. Now we get to repair it with self awareness and choices. These lists will help us take back our power to create lives that are a reflection of our inner world.

19 ~ RELATIONSHIPS, CHOICES, AND SELF HELP

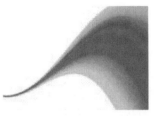

Though passing time ferried us out of our childhood sexual abuse, many of us continue to feel stuck in the same current. In the river of life, we feel unable to paddle to new possibilities for happiness.

It's the most natural thing in the world to float downstream, using the same skills that helped us survive. We might numbly accept persistent, upsetting rapids because we don't know how to use our oars of personal power to guide us safely around them. Maybe we learned to blindly swim in any direction as long as it was away from our circumstance, and we're still doing that today. Many of us continue to fill every moment with activity so we don't hear the turbulent waters of our secret.

We endured by learning how to cope, but we also diminished our ability to identify rich relationships that would feel like rainbows in our life. To find those, we can use self awareness. There is empowering magic in beginning a conscious adventure of making a list of the qualities we need, enjoy, appreciate, and must have to feel joyous in a relationship.

My list includes descriptions of characters in books and movies, people I barely know, and those I love. When I experience something that makes my spirit sing, I add it to my treasure of words. I can witness an interaction and know I want some of that included. Mother Nature, animals, and the beauty of things can inspire me.

This list is a powerful tool for survivors. It asks us to focus on the good in the world around us. It feeds our sense of well-being. This conscious connection to what we want will begin guiding our choices about who we want in our life. Our abuse taught us how relationships can be, but our list will show us who will fill our hearts.

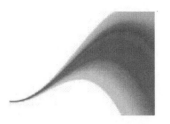

20 ~ SELF HELP TAKES COURAGE

Survivors of child abuse didn't explore the landscape of childhood; they hunted for paths that might avoid landmines of harm. Whether they tip-toed with caution or brought their guns of anger, their primary focus was getting through another day. Secrets and survival were the guiding forces. Personal growth was the friend you didn't bring home.

Back then, the child-we-were didn't have a parent who could help us become our full potential. But, today, we can become that caring, empowering adult for the child that still lives within us… who is still a voice in our head as we make choices. By connecting to that part of ourselves, we can transform that inner child experience, and that will change how we feel today.

This isn't about remembering. It's about using techniques like EFT (Emotional Freedom Technique), guided imagery, journaling, and hypnotherapy to deeply "be" that child once again. Then the spirit of that child can be as much a part of our days as the other people in our lives. When we connect at this level, we not only learn what they need, know, and feel, we gain tremendous insight into what shaped our beliefs.

We can nurture, encourage, celebrate, and guide, giving this child what they didn't have growing up. We can do this time and time again, with different ages, until we have an army of inner children who helped us survive.

And each time we connect, we can honor them for all their choices. We can appreciate the many ways they helped us get through the war of our childhood so we would have the chance to explore our possibilities in peace.

21 ~ FIND THE WORDS TO HEAL

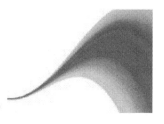

FINDING THE WORDS…ALWAYS TRYING TO FIND THE WORDS TO SAY WHAT I FEEL. I DON'T KNOW HOW TO SAY THE WORDS YET. I AM DRIVEN TO PUT WORDS TOGETHER, TO TELL THE STORY IN DIFFERENT WAYS, EXPLORING IT FROM DIFFERENT ANGLES. BUT ALWAYS ON PAPER OR ON THE SCREEN. MY MOUTH CAN'T YET SAY WHAT I WRITE.   ~ Robin Bond

Reading Robin's words, my heart beat the familiar, erratic rhythm from my healing journey. Finding my voice to describe my experience was the key to moving out of the shadowed forests of childhood sexual abuse, but they were elusive for three reasons.

I couldn't talk about the moments of my abuse, because those memories weren't processed like ordinary memories. They were taken directly to the primitive part of my brain through my senses and emotions. I smelled the moment. I saw minute details as my fears and confusion roared through my body, but they were never taken to the part of my brain that holds descriptions. My memories were stored in unshed tears. They hid behind my aversion to certain odors.

As I struggled to find the words, I was like Robin. The first stop was often in black letters on white paper because every cell in my body was still warning me to keep the secret. And when I dared to share the bits and pieces of the story that came to me, I was often deeply embarrassed to share images I was only beginning to comprehend. I was once again the child and the words were naughty, icky, and nasty.

My adult self could say them, but the child who was connected to the moment stammered, stuttered, and stretched to share her truth.

Words were also elusive because they were the ladder out of my deep hole of denial. I resisted what would reveal my truth… as though that would make it go away. Silence was a way of postponing action, setting new boundaries, and accepting my abuse really did happen.

FINDING THE WORDS…. They will take survivors to their truth. And they often hide in the fog of our experience.

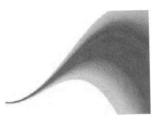

22 ~ PRINCESS

No matter how whole we appear to others, survivors of trauma memories know it's an illusion. We feel like a shadow of our self, not the princess we present to the world. When we look in the mirror, we don't see what others see. Compliments and praise are swallowed by the abused child's shame before the adult can taste the wonder of being something good. Many of us hesitate to step forward with our personal talents and gifts because the dark side dims our inner light.

We are inclined to hide from others. Whether we've dissociated our memories or pushed them into the corners of our mind, we instinctively know getting truly close could expose our secret self. We might be the friendly person with no close friends, the quiet one on the fringes, the always-giving and nurturing paragon, or the boisterous one who needs control in every situation. Our disguises come in many shapes. They reflect how we learned to manage the roaring pain of having who we are distorted by what we experienced.

With our true self tangled in the web of our abuse, survivors are challenged to connect to their inner wisdom and perceptions. Rather than connecting to the empowering knowledge of our personal spirit, we learned how to exist by responding to our abuser. The guiding force of our insights got lost as we denied what we knew or felt. To keep our secret, our truth could not be embraced.

We leave our abusers in the past, but we very naturally build our futures with our built-in need to react rather than take action on our own behalf. We shape our lives with the lessons we learned and continue believing this is WHO WE ARE.

Healing is a journey to discover who we are without the shadow of who we became to survive.

23 ~ ROAD TO RECOVERY

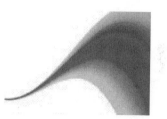

Our healing journey begins in the deep, dark, and intimidating forests of our experience where no path is visible. The road to recovery becomes paved with insights over time.

Finding our way to the sunny meadows of our lives is a daunting adventure of self-empowerment, but we don't have to travel alone. Since sexual abuse was first declared a "crime" in literature of the 80's, many allies have armed themselves with knowledge, compassion, and tools for helping us.

We have to point the direction with each step we take, but therapists, survivor groups, and books can provide light. Body work, energy insights, healing touch, shaman ceremonies, hand analysis, and other healings of heart and spirit are also allies. Only we can choose the pace or who we will invite into our circle of support. That choice is part of our healing. It defines us and calls on us to trust our inner wisdom.

Although abuse left us feeling powerless in so many ways, we do take this journey with a bag of personal tools for healing. Our inner wisdom is a glowing ember, and each time we trust our instincts it becomes a stronger friend. The courage that helped us survive is like a cape, always there to wrap around us when we need its warmth. Feelings are our compass. A sandwich of hope and determination is there to nourish us.

Healing asks us to create a map when we feel utterly lost, but others are leaving clues along the way if we choose to use them. And there are treasures along the way. Every time we embrace the insights that come with seeing our past experience through the lens of our current circumstance, we release what has held us captive. Old reality shifts to a new perspective. Change happens. Step by step, we find ourselves living in a different world, leaving the dark forest behind.

24 ~ CHOOSING TO

REACH OUT

As my dog looked up from our morning cuddle and saw her shadow, I felt the Universe give me a gift of insight. This is what it feels like to carry trauma memories... dark images skirting around the edges of our sunshine.

She barked at the scary interruption in her day. Those of us who have experienced childhood sexual abuse often avoid the shadows of our past. We shy away, deny, and run toward busy, hoping to ignore the darkness of our experience. But, as any sunny moment will remind you, the shadows are still there. The fear remains until we turn toward the memories, walk into them, and merge our experience with our current self.

Twenty-two years after my healing journey began, I chose to reach out to others with words. As I wrote, SPIRIT UNBROKEN: ABBY'S STORY, *I WAS TRYING TO BRING LIGHT TO SEXUAL ABUSE.* I wanted readers to understand the trauma memories of PTSD (Post Traumatic Stress Disorder) with their emotions and senses. I hoped to take them to a deeper understanding of the experience that affects so many. I wanted to empower people who support survivors in their healing. I believed I could open doors of insight for those who just can't imagine that all memories are not the same.

Whether Abby's story feels like a life raft, turbulent white waters, or a novel that "explained dissociation better than anything," we are all moved forward in our journeys of self-empowerment with information. And, I believe, we save another child every time we talk about something that can only thrive in secrecy.

Books were my life raft during my first three years of healing. Before the Internet offered its depth of support, authors had begun stepping forward with their insights, research, and knowledge. They made all the difference.

I wanted to make a difference, too.

25 ~ MEMORIES REVEALING THEMSELVES

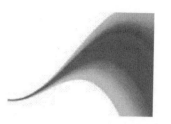

An *ordinary memory* sits like a photograph in a family album. It's always available to visit by thumbing through the album. A *trauma memory* is not pasted in the photo album. It's relegated to the attics of our mind to be stored in the unconscious. *Dissociation* happens when a trauma memory is ripped into pieces and locked in a vault without our knowing the photo was taken.

My childhood had trauma memories, those events I could remember but didn't want to think about. They rarely intruded, but sometimes I would go to that attic in my mind to pull out a past memory and stumble across them. Like sorting through a box of photos collecting dust, my memories were jumbled together, a happy moment right next to a distressing event that was associated with it in some way.

It was the dissociated memories that shocked and then challenged me. I hadn't known they existed. I didn't know there was a vault that would safely store the kind of trauma memories that were so overwhelming, disempowering, and life-threatening that I couldn't manage them as a child. I didn't know I was a survivor of PTSD.

Shock turned to challenge as I gathered information and embraced a healing journey with an outstanding therapist who knew the landscape of dissociated memories and childhood sexual abuse. At first, it felt like haunting, scary, ugly ghosts emerging from a "secret room" in my mind without my permission. When I fully embraced my journey of healing, they became empowering snapshots from my past.

Each time I surrendered to the memories that were bubbling up, I came away with gifts that helped me reshape by life in ways that thrilled me. They could show me moments that had transformed personal choices into coping reactions. These memories had information about fears that defined my days, relationships that did not honor my spirit, and feelings I didn't understand. They had the power to shine a light on habits I couldn't change even though they didn't serve me.

Inviting secrets that were held in my subconscious to protect me was a maze-like experience. In this landscape of sharp corners, dead ends, and no paths, I was moving past resistance and into the arms of healing. Then I wished the secrets weren't held so securely and deeply inside because I wanted to know the treasures found in the answers they held.

26 ~ SIX-YEARS OLD AND NO ONE LISTENS

Survivors of childhood sexual abuse are bound to bump into the howling, painful recognition of being alone in their experience. There was no protection… no soft, understanding place to go when they needed it the most.

In healing, this realization opens the door to many layers of feelings. There is tremendous value in walking into them so they can be processed rather than pushed away. This is our chance to see how our anger, frustration, pain, isolation, grief, and other emotions have spread into our current lives, affecting our relationships. It's a pond to swim through to get to the other side where our past no longer defines our future.

Seeking answers and insights means we won't end up floating in these feelings indefinitely. Working with a therapist, journaling, reading, EFT, and energy work are a few of the ways we can build rafts to navigate this deep pool of emotions. Each survivor finds their own way, knowing the quality of their life depends on it.

After I realized the six-year-old inside me STILL needed what my parents hadn't given me, I took a giant step forward in my healing journey. I became that inner child's parent. I recognized it wasn't too late, and I had the power to be everything that child within me needed so she could feel whole, loved, and empowered.

As I began taking care of my abused six-year-old, I felt the waves of healing wash into every part of my adult life. I was building a solid boat to cross my pond of feelings.

We are survivors. We are also the perfect, understanding, protective, caring parent our inner *CHILDREN* need right now.

27 ~ HEALING PROCESS

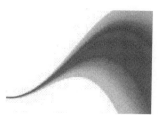

Healing from childhood sexual abuse felt like a cavalcade of challenges, obstacles, rewards, insights, emotions, and the incomprehensible. Though every survivor can recognize this landscape, each of us has our own experience. This is what I learned about healing from dissociated trauma memories.

~ It always brings us the experiences, people, and opportunities we need.

~ The rewards are immediate and a constant part of the journey.

~ Going back INTO the memory allows us to discover what we learned in that trauma. It empowers us to update old beliefs and feelings, and this changes our lives.

~ Trauma memories are laid down through emotions and our five senses. Going back into them gives us a chance to put the experience into words, and this is essential to healing.

~ In reconnecting to our personal spirit, we find paths to honor and celebrate ourselves. We connect to inner wisdom and perceptions rather than coping mechanisms.

~ Healing is about discovering we have choices and learning how to take care of ourselves with those choices.

~ It shows us how to respond rather than ignore. It gives us tools to take action instead of reacting.

Healing requires courage, the same courage that got each of us through the trauma of sexual abuse. We still have that courage... much to our surprise.

Recognizing our memories are not the enemy, we can embrace them as protective allies and clues to our well-being. Even though there are many times we think we aren't able, don't deserve, can't imagine, wouldn't dare, or couldn't possibly take the next step in healing, I invite you to dig deep and keep trying. There are gifts of joy waiting for you.

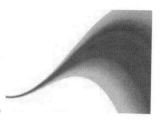

28 ~ CAN'T STAND THE PAIN, LEAVE

In the ordinary events of life, I didn't know my mind had the amazing ability to protect me. That understanding came to me during my healing journey from childhood sexual abuse. And it brought a conflict.

I moved through motherhood not knowing parts of my youth were carefully held in my unconscious, completely out of my reach to recall. When the memories of my past began showing up in my days, I didn't know if they were my enemy… or my savior.

Each memory turned my very average life upside-down and inside-out. It might leak out over several weeks, kidnapping my routines one-by-one until I could pull all the revelations together and comprehend an event from the past. Or the memory could rip me out of a sound sleep as an ordinary dream twisted into an experience from my childhood. Either way, my emerging trauma memory felt like a thief, stealing time out of my days and robbing my capacity to take charge of my life.

In this time of personal upheaval, I eventually realized I had an opportunity. When I didn't fight this adversary, when I chose to turn and embrace the information being revealed, the darkness became beacons of light. Each piece of emerging memory was truly just the messenger. I was being given the chance to understand what had happened to me, to find words to describe it, and then update the information so I was no longer a captive in the long-ago event.

In the trauma moments of my childhood, when I felt beyond fearful and emotionally overwhelmed, I had to leave. My mind did that for me when it dissociated the memory of the abuse. This natural, primitive response was a savior. Dissociation made it possible for me to experience my growing-up years. And the memories that felt so intrusive as they made themselves known to me were not the enemy. They were gifts to help me find my way back to my self.

29 ~ YOU FIND THE SECRETS

DEEP INSIDE

My first memory of childhood sexual abuse blew my world into a million fragments. I was 42 and felt like everything I KNEW about my life was now scattered at my feet like pieces of a puzzle that needed to be put back together again.

As I clung to the book, COURAGE TO HEAL, like a life raft, worked with a therapist, and staggered forward on my healing journey, I realized the puzzle I was putting back together didn't look like the familiar picture of my past. I recognized you find secrets deep inside when you have dissociated trauma memories.

While it's crazy-making to have flashes of your unknown past pop up without warning, it's just as frustrating to be ready and determined to reclaim your truth and not be able to remember by following the usual path of memories. In one of those moments, when I was feeling washed away by a river of emotion, I grabbed my pen and started drawing lines until I understood; my sexual abuse memories would not come until I was ready.

My mind had tenderly pulled them out of my awareness and stored them in a secret room to protect me during my abuse and it was continuing to protect me. This drawing helped me understand my job was not LOOKING FOR THE MEMORIES, but doing everything possible to feel safe, empowered, and ready for the information held deep inside.

I could invite insights, and I did, but my days were spent building the foundation for what I would learn when a memory came. I resisted feeling I was on my own by actively responding to the security of my daily routines, the few allies who believed and cared about my experience, my survivors' group, and my empowering, excellent therapist. I read everything I could find, and I wrote in my healing journal without fail. I began being consciously aware of trusting my inner wisdom about the little things so I could rely on that feeling when the deeply embedded truths came out.

I didn't know it then, but all these choices were part of the puzzle I was putting together. Memories give us valuable insights and bring changes, but we are also finding those pieces of ourselves that can take action to support our well-being.

30 ~ GOING TO FEELINGS

Every moment of our childhood abuse asked us to manage the incomprehensible. Without personal power, we had to withstand what shamed, frightened, hurt, confused, and sometimes threatened our lives. One tool most survivors used was shutting down their feelings.

After the abuse, these feelings might come out in their every-day lives as "anger at everything," recurring depression, or schedules so full there is no time to think. There are as many reactions to shutting down feelings as there are survivors. For me, it was hiding behind a smile. This was the safe place I chose to build my life.

It worked well for me. Feelings from my abuse were blocked from my awareness by a thick wall of suppression. But years later, when my first memory broke through, feelings from my past crowded into the same elevator I was taking to healing. I could feel them breathing down my neck.

One afternoon, I paced around my living room, shaking. Like a zombie, I moved through the quiet house while my kids were at school and my husband at work. Four months into therapy, I knew my sexual abuse was the reason. I had no idea why I was in this state, but I chose to stay there rather than crawl away from it by getting busy or reading.

That choice opened the door to understanding. It took me to a piece of paper, ruler, and black pen. It was the beginning of using these expressive friends to "see" what I was experiencing.

Drawing converging black lines to a point on the paper, I recognized I believed my feelings would take me into a black hole, and I truly did not know if I would come back out. I was scared I would get lost in an unending darkness of feelings and wouldn't find my way back to my life.

But healing journeys give us gifts of insight. I drew a small circle heading into the void. That was me. Then I drew another circle nearby. I didn't have to go in alone… and that made all the difference.

31 ~ WHY CHILDREN DON'T TELL

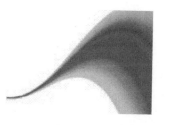

Children don't typically talk about the bad things happening at home.

I don't recall one conversation in my grade school classroom, on the playground, in Blue Birds, or riding bikes after school that included a discussion about how our parents treated us. We didn't play hopscotch in the dirt while our friend told us about her daddy drinking, swearing, and hitting. No one ever stop swimming at the park so they could share being scared of their parents.

Most children are unwilling to betray their family secrets. They don't want to share what feels deeply shameful. I have walked beside many survivors on their healing journey and this is one of the biggest hurdles. To stand up and say, "I was betrayed by a person I trusted to take care of me." They are unable to destroy the connections and images held by their family. It's challenging for adult survivor to say it. For most children, it is nearly impossible.

So much of why a child can't speak up about their sexual abuse is rooted in what they have learned about being part of a family. You are loyal, you obey, you respond, you get along, and you do your part to hold your family together no matter what.

When I watch parents insist on their children kissing other adults goodnight, I know the groundwork is being laid for that child to feel driven to respond when any adult in the extended family circle approaches them. Why would a child tell about an occurrence that starts feeling icky or intimidating, but is part of family expectations?

I see this and I don't know the answer for saving a child from sexual abuse, but I know the solution is not in telling them to "say no" or "go tell someone." That places the burden on the small shoulders of the very person who is already disempowered by age. Even more, it asks the person who is emotionally battered, confused, and afraid to step forward and shatter the illusion of family truth. It asks too much.

As a survivor of sexual abuse, I have looked at this question for the children in my life. How could I create the opportunity for them to break through the wall of silence that could hold them prisoner to abuse? My answer is this: believe them. Believe the tiniest whisper of truth they can share.

Believe a child who doesn't want to be around an uncle for no apparent reason. Accept the possibility if your child won't ride their bike by the house of that nice neighbor who is always working in the vegetable garden and sharing the bounty. Recognize 1 of-3 girls is sexually abused and 1 of-5 boys is molested… and 90% of the abusers are well-known by their family. Acknowledge those who entice or threaten these children are just like the people you know, have met, share time with, and could be part of your family.

Black-Ink Insights

Finding ways to quiet our thoughts can take us to the information we hold deep inside. For me, that path opened up on a quiet afternoon when I desperately needed to "see" what I was "feeling."

I picked up a black pen, ruler, and sheets of typing paper and sat down at my coffee table. At that time in my life, I would have told you I didn't have a creative bone in my body. I had no plan, no idea why I was sitting there. I only knew my need to understand what was happening to me was stronger than my fears.

Instinct must have guided me, because I drew black lines on the white paper without knowing where they would go or why each line felt it was emerging in just the right place. While tears of release fell, my fingers moved, and my mind watched in silent acceptance.

The sometimes frantic, sometimes slow, fluid strokes came to an end when I had gone fully, completely into my feelings and out the other side. That's when I saw what had been happening on the paper. That's when the words came to describe what I was expressing and the picture had a title.

I felt incredibly empowered. That afternoon, when I followed my spirit and sat down with a pen, ruler, and paper, I found a way to listen to my body's wisdom. It became my ally during my healing journey.

Sometimes images take us to a place words can't. The following images are my black-ink insights ~ Jeanne

"The Power of Art in Healing"

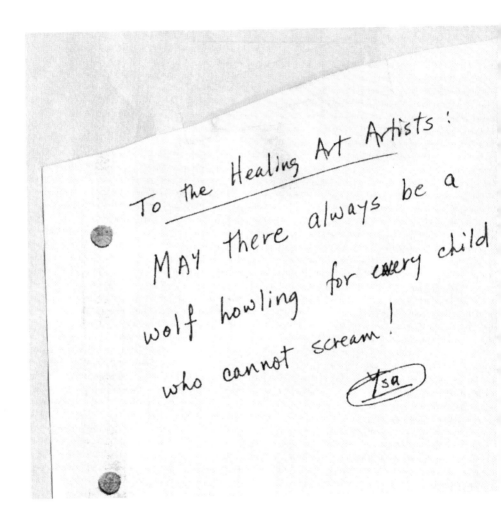

Ink Insight 1 ~ Going To Feelings

Going to Feelings

Ink Insight 2 ~ You Find the Secrets Deep Inside

You Find the Secrets Deep Inside

Ink Insight 3 ~ Six-Years Old and No One Listens

Six-Years Old and No One Listens

Ink Insight 4 ~ It Doesn't "Just Go Away"

It Doesn't 'Just Go Away'

Ink Insight 5 ~ Road to Recovery

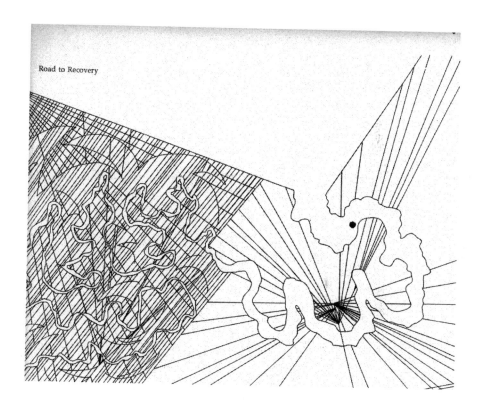

Road to Recovery

Ink Insight 6 ~ My Sea of Black Tears

My Sea of Black Tears

Ink Insight 7 ~ Releasing Guilt

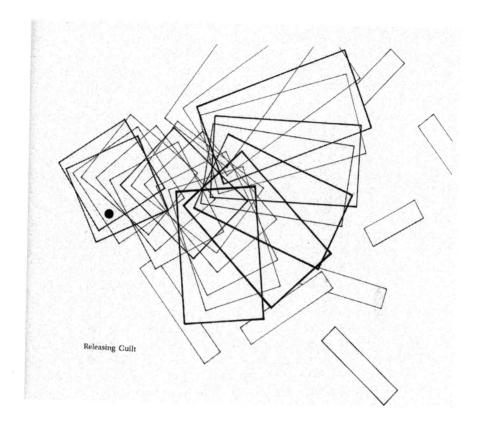

Releasing Guilt

Princess *Chelan*

Ink Insight 9 ~ Memories Revealing Themselves

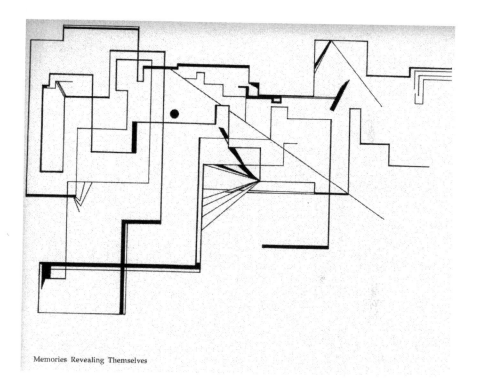

Memories Revealing Themselves

Ink Insight 10 ~ Anger

Anger

Ink Insight 11 ~ Healing Process

Healing Process

Confusion

Ink Insight 13 ~ I'm More Than My Abuse

I'm More Than My Abuse

This is what you saw

this is what I am

Ink Insight 14 ~ Can't Stand the Pain, Leave

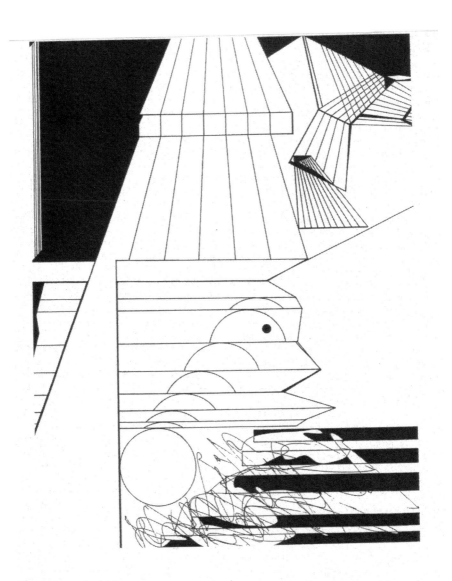

Can't Stand the Pain, Leave

Ink Insight 15 ~ The Other Side of Healing

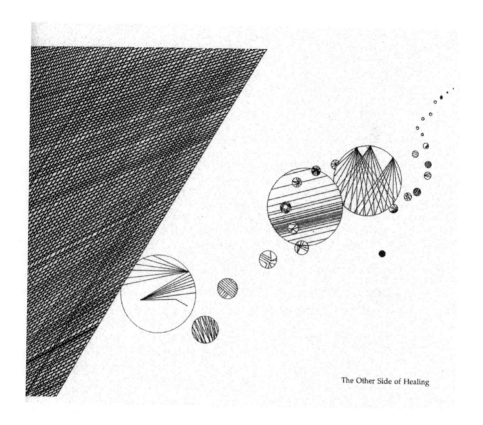

The Other Side of Healing

More Books: Amazon.com
Author website: GoToSpirit.com
Author blogs: "Sexual Abuse Insights"
                  "Guided by Personal Spirit"
                  "Talking to Energy"
Author YouTube: Jeanne McElvaney
Contact: jeanne@gotospirit.com

Made in the USA
Charleston, SC
24 January 2014